CAN NEOLIBERALISM BE SAVED FROM ITSELF?

COLIN CROUCH

SOCIAL EUROPE EDITION

Chapter 1

WHAT'S WRONG WITH NEOLIBERALISM?

For many people in or around Britain the sight of the burning hulk of the Grenfell Tower block of flats in Kensington, London during the night of 14 June 2017 was the final horrific comment on the ideology that had guided so much public policy for the previous four decades. A small fire in one apartment spread rapidly throughout the block, probably killing around 100 people; the true figure will probably never be known. Whatever the role of the recently installed cladding on the block played in spreading the fire, and why a form of cladding had been used that is banned in Germany, the USA and some other countries, we have also yet to learn. But there was a strong suspicion that the decision to use it was motivated by public spending cost considerations. Residents in the block had indicated their concerns about the cladding 19 times to their local authority, the Royal Borough of Kensington and Chelsea, but had received no response. Like most local authorities in the United Kingdom, the borough had handed over management of its properties and many of its other services to private companies with a mandate to maximise their shareholders' profits rather than provide services of a specific quality. In the hours and days after the fire, masses of volunteers came to the aid of the distraught and now homeless residents, as did the public fire, police and medical services. But there was virtually no sign of care workers from the local authority. By early August only ten families of the hundreds who had been living in the block had been rehoused. Kensington and Chelsea is the richest borough in London, and one of the richest residential areas in the world; large numbers of apartments and houses within it are left empty, owned by very wealthy people from around the world, who either use them very occasionally or keep them merely for their investment value.

Kensington and Chelsea council is dominated by the Conservative Party, the main political exponent of neoliberal ideas in the UK. Many of its wealthy residents draw their incomes from the financial sector that dominates the British economy and whose success is an example of neoliberalism at work. It is central to neoliberal ideas that public spending must be kept to a minimum, including spending on social care services; that health and safety regulation should be the butt of sceptical jokes; and that residual public services should be provided by profit-maximising firms, as these will be more efficient than a local authority's own employees. The residents of Grenfell Tower were tenants of social housing. In an ideal neoliberal world there would be no social housing; people would live in whatever they could afford within the private market, irrespective of the quality. Under the influence of these ideas, successive UK governments and councils of all parties have gradually run down the stock of social housing. (In 1981 32% of English homes were in such accommodation and 11% in privately rented homes – the remainder were owner-occupied. By 2016 the social housing figure had dropped to 7%, private renting had risen to 31%.) Social housing tenants are the unwanted residue of a pre-neoliberal past.

Neoliberalism also celebrates inequality, which is interpreted as reflecting the appropriate rewards of market-related economic activity. If people consider themselves to be too poor, then they should see that as an incentive to work harder. One's level of income and wealth is therefore an indicator of one's social worth. A council like that of Kensington and Chelsea would not have a great deal of respect for residents of a place like Grenfell Tower.

These and many other instances of the negative consequences of a low tax, low regulation regime, with high inequality and lack of concern for collective needs have led many people to reject the whole neoliberal adventure; certainly to see the political and business leaders who have embraced it so whole-heartedly over the decades as incapable of saving it from its self-made disasters. For others, however, there is much that has been attractive about its vision of a world where people can keep almost everything that they earn without a proportion being taken in taxes; where one can therefore spend one's money as one chooses, rather than have governments spend it on things in which one might have no interest; where official rules and regulations interfere with life as little as possible; where businesses are left free to plan how they can best make a profit, generating wealth that gradually spreads to everyone. At the heart of the vision is the pure market, a place where everyone expresses their preferences, those goods and services are produced for which there is popular demand, and no one dominates. The values of all the goods and services one might want to acquire can be compared through the market's prices. Every individual, firm and national economy freely and amicably trades and competes with each other, all doing what they do best and benefiting from each other's contributions.

Is it impossible to keep many of the advantages that a free market economy can deliver, while also maintaining a welfare state, redistributive taxation and a degree of regulation to rein in the excesses of a system aimed solely at the maximisation of profit and individual material gain, generating extreme inequalities on the way? In practice, the answer has to be 'yes', because in no advanced economy, even that of the US, where neoliberal ideas are especially dominant, has the neoliberal vision been realised in its entirety. Social spending, progressive taxation and regulation survive and keep returning after attempts to hack them back. In real politics rather than in the battle of ideas, the debate between neoliberals and their critics is a matter of degree: not whether to retain or destroy the rival institutions at stake, but what balance to achieve among them.

I am writing for those who feel that, even if there is some element of compromise in place, neoliberalism has gone too far in making society unequal and in allowing those values that can be pursued through the market to dominate over others. How might the balance be redressed? That it *could* be redressed is clear: there is no shortage of ideas, practical policies and national examples for more equitable ways of having a competitive market economy that also achieves a high level of social justice. The problem is one of power and will. The world's great corporations and super-rich individuals have major leverage over governments of all kinds, and they have a strong interest in low taxes (at least on the wealthy), poor public services (because they never use them) and low regulation of business activities. We need the jobs that the corporations create and the goods and services they produce. But the more wealth that they and rich individuals accumulate, the more resources they can deploy to influence governments; the more that they can influence governments, the more they can secure policies that suit their interests; the more they do that, the more wealth they accumulate; and thus the self-reinforcing spiral moves on. It seems that one can expect only an intensification of neoliberalism rather than its moderation. It is a bitter irony that this political process that entrenches neoliberalism is itself completely contrary to neoliberalism's own principles, according to which there should be no political lobbying for economic ends.

But cracks have been appearing in neoliberalism's glossy surface. The financial crash of 2007-8 was its very own crisis, and in recent years there have been growing signs of popular anger at neoliberalism's consequences in many countries. As Wolfgang Streeck has shown in *Buying Time*, the global economic system is becoming increasingly dependent on debt, public and private, which is reaching limits of sustainability. Some observers see here an imminent collapse of the entire neoliberal capitalist edifice. Some dream that this as an opportunity to create socialism, however that is defined in this post-Soviet age; others, including Streeck, warn that economic collapse could well lead to a far worse world than we experience now. It is therefore urgent to explore neoliberalism's capacity to accept reform. Are there points at which global corporations, the super-rich and governments under their influence would be likely to accept that they must change direction, or face recurrent crisis?

Various political forces have had to acknowledge this in the past. After the Second World War, European conservatives had to learn that their willingness to make alliances with Nazism and fascism in order to ward off mass democracy had been disastrous. They then became highly adept practitioners of the compromise strategy of conservative or Christian democracy. At various points starting in the 1950s the social democratic movements of Europe contemplated the ugly edifice that was being constructed in the name of socialist planning in the Soviet bloc. At different speeds and with different degrees of enthusiasm they came to realise that the market economy should be accepted, not just as a temporary compromise with political realities, but because, when combined with social democrats' own policies of strong social policy and government economic management, it produced a better world than state socialism was achieving in the east. A similar conversion is now required of neoliberals. If their ideology is to depart from the destructive path on which it is currently set, they must appreciate that such things as progressive taxes, a strong welfare state aimed at enhancing economic capacity, and business regulation that enables us to pursue goals other than narrow profit maximisation are positive in themselves and not just occasional temporary political necessities. There would still be many opportunities for conflict between neoliberals and their various (social democratic, green, social liberal and conservative) opponents. Agreement that, say, income inequalities need to be reduced still leaves considerable room for debate over how much, through what means and with what urgency.

For the past quarter century to call for the 'reform' of some institution or other has meant to make it more subject to the discipline of the market, to remove regulation, cut taxes and reduce the role of government in general. 'Reform' has come to be a euphemism for neoliberalism. Can the boot now be put on to the other foot, with neoliberal edifices being themselves subject to

a tough reform process? To be able to contemplate these
possibilities, neoliberalism's critics need to stop seeing it
as an undivided, rock-like and evil edifice. There are
major divisions among neoliberals, most importantly a
rarely noticed one between advocates of the pure
market and those who incongruously equate the market
with dominant corporations. There are also vulnerabili-
ties, in particular those that stem from neoliberalism's
role in the 2007-8 financial crisis, and those concerned
with its relationship to the nationalistic and xenophobic
forces that have today become important across much of
the world. On the other hand, some of neoliberalism's
achievements have been useful and should be retained.
These are the issues that I shall address in this book. It is
not a contribution to the demonology of neoliberalism,
but an attempt at a nuanced account. Only in that way
can we assess its capacity for reform. We must first
clarify the main characteristics of neoliberalism, and
what is wrong with it; then consider why it should not be
viewed solely negatively; and finally assess the capacity
of its protagonists to rescue it from what are emerging as
its self-destructive tendencies.

What is neoliberalism?

Neoliberalism is a political strategy that seeks to make as
much of our lives as possible conform to the economist's
ideal of a free market. That simple idea is all one really
needs to understand what it is about, and it has been the
ruling idea of most governments in the western world
and beyond for almost 40 years. There are several good

books for readers wanting a richer understanding. David Harvey's *A Brief History of Neoliberalism* offers a highly critical perspective. More balanced is *Neoliberalism* by Damien Cahill and Martijn Konings. Philip Mirowski goes deeper into the highly organised way in which leading neoliberal thinkers set about influencing government policy across the world in *Never Let a Serious Crisis Go to Waste*. Werner Bonefeld provides a similar analysis of the specifically German form of neoliberalism known as *Ordoliberalismus* in *The Strong State and the Free Economy*. In *The Limits of Neoliberalism* William Davies demonstrates how deeply neoliberal ideas have penetrated into the obsession with calculation and measurement in contemporary government.

Neoliberals believe strongly in a capitalist economy, one in which most wealth is in private hands and where market transactions dominate. But neoliberalism is not coterminous with capitalism; not all forms of the latter feature the total faith in markets and rejection of an economic role for government that we find in neoliberalism. We might define neoliberals as capitalist extremists. While it is common in contemporary political thought, especially in the US, to see capitalism and democracy as inseparably linked, many neoliberal and ordoliberal thinkers have in fact been highly suspicious of democracy, and have wanted to ensure that its ability to interfere with markets is highly restricted. This is well discussed by Bonefeld, Mirowski, and by Streeck in *Buying Time*.

The term was first coined by a group of mainly German and American economists and philosophers who wanted to avert what they thought would be the disasters of a socialist planned economy, or indeed of any role for government in the economy other than that of protecting capitalist competition itself. Based initially on an organisation called the Mont Pèlerin Society (named after a mountain in Switzerland), they grew in numbers and political importance and began to operate through a wide range of think tanks, such as, among many others (in the USA) the American Enterprise Institute, the Heritage Foundation and the Cato Institute; in the UK the Adam Smith Institute and the Institute for Economic Affairs. The World Economic Forum that meets every year at Davos in Switzerland was established to promulgate neoliberal ideas at a global level, though it allows expression of a wider range of views at its meetings than do most other neoliberal institutes. Neoliberals' opposition to government restraint on capitalist activity has attracted the heavy financial support of many wealthy interests opposed to government regulation of their activities. This is especially the case with the US oil industry, billionaires like the Koch brothers being active in funding neoliberal organisations and various neoliberal lobbying activities, including those related to climate change denial.

As their influence has come to dominate the world, and as their policies have attracted criticism, neoliberals have become coy about using the word. The key neoliberal texts appeared before the 1980s, the decade when, starting with Ronald Reagan in the USA and Margaret Thatcher in the UK, the ideology began to gain the active support of powerful political leaders. Friedrich von Hayek's *The Road to Serfdom* dates back to 1944, though Hayek himself lived on to become a close associate of Thatcher. Ayn Rand's *The Virtue of Selfishness* first appeared in 1964, though the Ayn Rand Institute formed in her memory remains active. Milton Friedman's two key ideological (as opposed to technical economic) works were published in 1962 (*Capitalism and Freedom*) and 1980 (with Rose Friedman, *Free to Choose*). Today neoliberalism is more likely to be named by its critics than by its apostles.

At the core of neoliberalism is a vision of the market as a mechanism that enables large numbers of individuals to express their free preferences. It gives incentives to producers of goods and services to meet those preferences, without the need for state regulation or commands; individuals need little from a wider society beyond a guaranteed capacity to express their wants through market choices. Neoliberals regard government as a particularly incompetent institution, the less of which we have, the better. The market is seen as self-correcting in a way that is more flexible and responsive than anything that can be achieved by government regulation. If consumers' tastes change, producers quickly notice this, stop producing goods and services that have become unpopular, and start producing what customers want. For example, if private home owners place a priority on fire protection and use their resources to acquire expensive cladding, then well and good; if they prefer to take the risk that a fire will occur and prefer to spend their money on other things, then that is their free choice too. No public issue arises; in the view of the most extreme neoliberals, there *are* no public issues. Similarly, if a firm starts to make defective or dangerous products, customers will notice this, and the firm will lose trade to honest practitioners. This can happen rapidly and without the need for elaborate rules and inspection services that a system of public regulation requires. All that is necessary is that the firm's sole role is made to be the realisation of maximum profit for its shareholders. Since, in a pure market, profits can be maximised only by satisfying customers, there is no need for customers' interests to be considered as any different from those of shareholders; there is therefore no need for consumer protection legislation. A major success of neoliberal reforms has been to have the maximisation of shareholder value made the sole legal object for firms in most advanced economies.

The weaknesses of the neoliberal approach can be analysed under five broad headings, at least four of which are fully recognised in the neoclassical economic theory on which neoliberalism draws. Economists, but not ideological neoliberals, are usually prepared to accept various forms of government intervention to remedy these market failures. The four are: the presence of negative externalities; the existence of public goods; the absence of means to counter systematic inadequacies in the information available to market participants;

and difficulties in achieving adequate cor
many sectors. Finally, where there is possib
ment with standard economics comes the fifth: ineq
ties in the ability of different people to participate fully
in the market.

Negative externalities are harmful by-products of market
activity, which do not form part of the costs of that
activity. The most obvious examples concern pollution.
In a free market, a firm suffers no financial cost if chem-
icals released from its factory chimneys damage the
health of large numbers of persons in the vicinity. Their
health is outside the market exchanges in which the firm
is engaged. This is a problem for neoliberals, who recog-
nise only those interests that are within the market,
arguing that considerations outside it cannot be calculated and therefore cannot be compared with those
within the market. They point out that even a polluting
economic activity adds to economic value, and that
simply suppressing the firm's activities or imposing taxation or expensive regulations on it might do more overall
harm than damaging the health of a few people. How
can we tell, if the latter is not part of the market? The
only solution they can see is for that health to be made
marketable, i.e. are the sick people willing to compensate
the firm's costs in abating the pollution? If not, then
they are deemed not to place a market value on their
own health adequate to pay for the constraints that
protecting it imposes on economic activity. Even if one
accepts that logic, it cannot cope with externalities
where the source cannot be linked to an identifiable

group of sufferers from it. This applies particularly strongly to the main environmental challenges resulting from economic activity facing us today, which affect billions of people and where there are no means for relating individual sources of pollution to individual damage. Such phenomena cannot be brought within the market. It is not surprising that many neoliberal think tanks are heavily engaged in climate change denial with devastatingly successful consequences for US rejection of international agreements on the issue.

Public goods are defined by economists to refer to goods (in the widest definition of that term as things that are desired) that are 'non-rival and non-excludable'. The first term means that the consumption by one person of a good does not prevent another person consuming it too; the second means that it is not possible to prevent people from having access to it. Non-rival goods lack a quality necessary if price to be set for them: scarcity, while if it is impossible to exclude people from the enjoyment of a good, it cannot be provided in the market. Therefore, in a pure market economy, public goods will not exist. If they are there already, as for example natural beauty spots, they are likely to be damaged or neglected, as no one has a market incentive to care for them. The only neoliberal solution is to impose an artificial scarcity and excludability by enforcing private ownership and enabling private owners to charge for access. This is often not practical (for example, fresh air or the ocean bed). Where it is possible, neoliberalism becomes a restrictive and controlling force rather than the liberating one that it is presented as being.

Problems of information: Economic theory assumes that market participants have perfect information – or at least as much information as they need – in order to make optimal decisions about the price, quality and other attributes of goods and services that they are buying and selling. It further assumes that rational actors will ensure that they have this, and therefore that, if we seem sometimes not to take much care in acquiring information before making a choice, then we can be assumed to have rationally concluded that we did not need to do so. But we often have very little chance of acquiring the knowledge we would need to make complex decisions. For example, can children or their parents be expected to know the value of education to them in twenty or thirty years' time? Similar arguments apply to decisions whether we ought to insure ourselves against illness, disability, unemployment, prolonged old age and other risks that might prevent us from earning a living. There are also many products that we buy in everyday markets, particularly technically complex ones, where it is extremely difficult for ordinary consumers to access adequate information to judge quality. Publicly funded provision of education and health care, and consumer protection legislation, are ways that we have found of tackling these problems. But public spending, public provision and regulation are anathema to neoliberals.

Inadequate competition: For markets to work the way that neoliberals need, there must be many producers and many consumers; no one producer or consumer should be in a position to influence the market price by its actions alone, and they must not conspire together to do so; it must also be easy for producers and consumers both to leave and enter the market. Absent these conditions, markets do not do their work of bringing producers and consumers together in ways that enable both to exercise choice while achieving overall efficiency. Real markets frequently lack one or more of these conditions. It might be practically impossible to have more than a small number of producers serving particular consumers, as with many public utilities. It might be difficult for new firms to enter, because of high start-up costs, or to leave (banks were defined in 2008 as being 'too big to fail', i.e. to leave the market). Some firms may be sufficiently large within a market to be able to manipulate prices. Further, if the condition of near-perfect competition is not fulfilled, then the neoliberal equivalence between shareholders' and customers' interests falls, as it becomes possible for firms to exploit market dominance. The shareholder maximisation model is then thrown into doubt.

Neoliberals here face a fundamental dilemma. Should they prioritise the maintenance of competition, and accept state intervention through competition law to ensure it, or prioritise keeping government out and therefore accepting restricted competition? As I have discussed in *The Strange Non-Death of Neoliberalism*, they divide over this in a highly important way. Advocates of the latter position claim that a competitive economy is one in which competition *has taken place*, producing winners, rather than one in which it is a *continuing* condition. This approach has gained dominance as neoliberals have come to depend on wealthy, often monopolistic corporations to fund their think tanks and lobbies. In the US in particular (less so in European Union (EU) competition law) neoliberal judges have watered down the previous emphasis of anti-trust law on maintaining competition. This change has required a redefinition of customers' interests from freedom to choose to the maximisation of their 'welfare'. This is in turn defined as indistinguishable from the overall wealth of a society, which is identified with the maximisation of profits. The theoretical equivalence between shareholders' and customers' interests has been restored in the absence of full competition, but by the sleight of hand of redefinition.

There is a further problem. Economic theory shows us that where competition is intense, profit rates are low. Firms must therefore be expected constantly to escape its constraints, boosting profits by exploiting monopoly positions – what economists call extracting 'rents'. This can be benign and describes how the market favours innovation: by doing something different from its rivals, a firm can escape their competition. After a while they imitate its success, the first mover's advantage is eroded, competition is restored, and firms in the sector look around for something new to try. But firms will be

seeking means to make first-mover advantages more
permanent. Generous patent and intellectual copyright
laws can help them do this, and so corporations
frequently lobby governments to intensify the protection
afforded by these laws. They can also benefit from what
are known as 'network externalities'. If a first mover can
develop a large network of contacts around its products,
competitor firms will have great difficulty rivalling it,
even if their products are superior. This is a long-term
problem, with important examples of large manufac-
turing companies that set up their own retail distribution
networks, making it difficult for rivals with better products but unable to set up chains of shops. But the Inter-
net, which is after all an epitome of networks, is creating
many more instances. Once a firm has reached a certain
size, it will always appear as the 'go to' site on the web.
Serious monopolies are being created in this way, and
some individuals are being made extremely rich.
Amazon, Google and Facebook are the most prominent
names among them, but there are many others. The
European Court of Justice, which has a strong neoliberal
mandate in this field, works at trying to find solutions to
the problem, but that takes time and is far from easy to
achieve. Some very important sectors of the modern
economy fall far short of the pure competition model
required by pure neoliberalism.

Similar problems have been created by a further ironical
twist. A major success of neoliberal reforms has been
the privatisation of many previously public services
(such as railways, postal services, gas, electricity and

water distribution) and the sub-contracting to private firms of others that continue to be publicly financed (such as health, education and elderly care). In most cases these services remain monopolies or with extremely restricted competition, and/or of deep public interest. Government therefore remains closely interested in them. The net result is nothing like a system of perfect markets; rather, a small circle of politically privileged 'crony' firms grows up, which specialise in getting government contracts and developing close political links. In the UK a small group of firms has become so central to public service delivery that, even though several of them have been fined for various offences against the terms of the contracts, they keep on winning new ones, because parts of the country's public services would collapse if they were no longer there. Like the banks during the financial crisis, they have become 'too big to fail' – a concept that is itself alien to the idea of a free market economy.

For these reasons I insist it is necessary to distinguish between 'market' and 'corporate' neoliberals. The former insist on trying to achieve perfect markets; the latter defend the role of oligopolistic corporations and therefore dilute the importance of the market. This makes them rather more realistic than market neoliberals, and pleases neoliberals' wealthy backers, but it fatally undermines the pure market condition and the entire rhetoric about customers' freedom to choose that remains a fundamental part of the case for neoliberalism and the sole justification for its central claim that maximising shareholders' profits also serves customers' interests better than any alternative.

Inequality: Neoclassical economics is ambiguous on the issue of inequality. It sees the pursuit of wealth as a fundamental motivation for economic behaviour, and therefore has to favour the inequalities of income and wealth that result from it. On the other hand, in a state of perfect competition, growing inequalities of income signal inadequate supply of the factor of production being rewarded. This should lead to an increase in supply of that factor until the inequality is reduced. For example, growing incomes among investment bankers should lead to more people becoming investment bankers, which should then reduce their incomes. A perfect market economy is therefore one in which inequalities keep rising *and falling*. Further, if inequalities are to act as incentives to effort, there should not be inheritance of wealth, as the second generation has not had to expend effort to secure its reward. We should expect a difference in approach to inequality among the different types of neoliberal. Market neoliberals should be dissatisfied with the incessantly growing inequalities that characterise the present period; corporate neoliberals, who have relinquished insistence on constant competition, will be very relaxed about it. The fact that neoliberals very rarely express concern at rising inequality suggests that the corporate form of the ideology has become dominant.

Inequality is highly relevant to the role of markets, as ability to use them depends on wealth. One can only accept that individuals' access to goods, services, information, and protection from limited externalities should be entirely constrained by their income and wealth if one is content that existing inequalities in their distribution can be justified. The more arbitrary that distribution, the less acceptable becomes reliance on the market. Further, although neoliberals will insist that the market is not concerned with moral worth, only efficiency, in reality high income is often taken as a sign of social and even moral superiority. The rich receive deference and respect in daily life in a manner never accorded to people on modest incomes. In a society where neoliberal values dominate, a hedge fund director will always receive far more real respect in everyday life than a hospital nurse, whatever ritual gestures are made to the latter.

Conclusion: What's wrong with neoliberalism

Neoliberalism is unable to cope with the externalities that, especially in the form of climate change, have become one of the gravest dangers confronting human life. It produces a society impoverished of public goods. It fails to equip citizens with the information they need to participate in the markets that it insists are the only fully acceptable form of allocation and decision-making. It has itself been corrupted by the rise of giant corporations, whose cause many neoliberals support even though this undermines the efficiency of the market itself. Finally, it offers no remedies for the inequalities produced by this distortion of its own pure form. It is not surprising that neoliberalism has many critics; and that, despite its dominance, almost nowhere has it been totally triumphant.

This is the pass to which the neoliberal revolution has brought us. Deregulation has enabled intensive industrial activity to damage the planet, perhaps to a point of no return. The growth of inequality has made many medium- and lower-income citizens dependent on high levels of debt if they are to maintain the level of consumption needed to keep the capitalist economy going. A vicious spiral is in progress: increased inequality increases the power of capitalist interests to affect public policy; these public policy changes in turn further increase inequality; and so on. The political power of neoliberalism is advanced by this spiral, though at the same time the integrity of neoliberalism itself is damaged: the use of political power for economic ends is anathema to market neoliberalism, though very welcome to its corporate counterpart. Meanwhile, a damaged planet and static incomes threaten the viability of the capitalist system itself.

Chapter 2

BABIES IN THE NEOLIBERAL
BATHWATER

Many critics would argue that the impact of neoliberalism has become so negative that reform is inadequate, and that the entire approach of a market-driven economy must be replaced with a state-run one, or the invention of some other unspecified system. It is important to achieve some balance. Neoliberal rejection of regulation has certainly intensified problems of environmental damage and climate change; but the environmental record of industrial activities under state socialism was even worse. The disregard for the lives of the poor demonstrated around the Grenfell Tower disaster was perpetrated by representatives of London's neoliberal financial elite; but contempt for ordinary people is standard practice among powerful groups of every kind. We also need to reflect on the positive contributions that the neoliberal approach has made. These can be summarised as: the discipline of price and calculation; helping us appreciate the limitations of democratic government; facilitating trade and reducing barriers to it; and facilitating links among people.

The discipline of price and calculation

Nearly everything we do has a cost, even if it is only what economists call 'opportunity cost' - the fact that doing one thing excludes doing certain other things. If I decide to spend money on a new coat, I need to consider not only the money value of the coat, but the things that I shall not be able to buy because I bought the coat. It is important that we do not regard actions as costless, particularly when calling for governments to spend money. While neoliberals are extreme in maintaining that governments' use of money will always, virtually by definition, be inferior to uses of it in the private market, it is entirely reasonable that government's spending choices are scrutinised and subject to open debate.

It is similarly important that, once it is agreed that there should be some government spending, it should be spent efficiently. Neoliberals claim that, because public services are not subject to competitive pressure, they are unlikely to be as concerned as private firms to ensure that they keep costs as low as possible. This is a serious argument. Although they have been unsuccessful in getting rid of public services and have been responsible for the anti-market forms of privatisation and sub-contracting that have often disfigured public service delivery, neoliberals have been responsible for many measures to ensure that public services resolve this problem, thereby often contributing to improvements in them and making them less vulnerable to neoliberals' own criticisms. Under a system known as new public management, public services have been submitted to performance measurement and needs to achieve targets, similar to those confronting firms facing pressures in the market. This has had some bad distorting effects, as when schools teach children only how to get high scores in targeted tests rather than impart knowledge to them. On the other hand, it has had some beneficial effects in making managers and professionals in these services consider what their objectives are, and be aware of a need to provide value for money.

A neoliberal approach also involves encouraging private individuals to think about the value of money and therefore about investing rather than spending. For example, in 2005 the British Labour government introduced Child Trust Funds, with the aim of introducing the ideas of savings and investment in financial markets among children. The government allocated £250 to every child born on or after 1 September 2002, with an additional £250 to children in low-income families. The money had to be kept in tax-free interest-earning savings schemes until the child reached 18 years, when various options were available. The child's family could contribute further funds. The objective was to encourage poorer families to become involved in investment, and the government planned to include financial planning in school curricula. The idea has clear neoliberal inspiration, encouraging young citizens to become involved in market risk management and to see themselves as market actors. But it was not pure neoliberalism, because it involved an initial egalitarian investment by the government. In 2011 the incoming Conservative-Liberal Democrat government improved the purity of the neoliberalism by abolishing the government subsidy.

The limitations of democratic government

Neoliberalism has also had a salutary impact on the tendency of politicians and public alike, especially but not only those on the socialist and social democratic left, to expect too much from government and its claims to democratic legitimacy. For example, a major neoliberal reform has been to have central banks made independent of government. This has been strongly criticised from the left on the grounds that it limits the ability of politicians to choose how high they will allow both inflation and public debt to rise. But this assumes a model of politics in which governments always serve the public interest. But politicians' strongest interest is in being re-elected. Allowing public debt to rise in order simultaneously to increase public spending on popular projects and keep taxes low is a perfect example of how they might achieve this, while inflicting long-term damage on the economy. The independence of central banks is designed to prevent precisely this kind of behaviour. Central bank independence is not a denial of democracy, but a protection of the public from its political manipulation.

Below we shall find good reason to criticise neoliberalism for being unable to cope with long-term issues. But, sadly, the same is also true of the democracy of representative government. Just as we need public policy to protect us from neoliberalism's deficiencies, some neoliberal institutions can also protect us from excessive expectations of how far governments can manipulate economic variables – and whether, when they do, they always act in our interest.

Facilitating trade and reducing barriers

When governments play a dominant role in deciding what goods and services their citizens produce and purchase, they are tempted to protect domestic producers from foreign competition, particularly by imposing tariffs and various rules to limit imports. This ensures stable employment, free from outside competition, for those producers. A particularly strong argument for protection is what is known as the 'infant industries' case. This assumes that a government or some firms in a country want to develop an activity in which others are already dominant. Only if the domestic industry is sheltered from competition for a period will it stand a

chance of becoming efficient enough in the longer run
to compete. A further reason for protection occurs when
competing countries are making goods and services far
more cheaply because they are exploiting labour or
allowing industries to damage the environment. If low
costs are always the key to competitiveness, there will be
a constant 'race to the bottom' of low standards, unless
countries with high labour and environmental standards
can protect themselves.

The neoliberal critique enables us to see some weaknesses in these arguments. First, how can it be guaranteed that protection will be used only for the purposes
stated? When will a government decide that an infant
industry has had enough protection and should now be
exposed to competition? How can one distinguish
between labour being exploited and labour being
cheaper simply because it is more efficient? Once
protectionist arrangements have been set up, close relations usually develop between government and the
leading firms in the industries concerned. The latter will
rarely propose the removal of protection, and will use
their good contacts with government to maintain it.
Consumers then face prices higher than necessary, and
the industries have little incentive to innovate, as their
domestic markets are protected from external competitors. When such industries are finally forced to give up
protection, and consumers are free to choose goods and
services on the open market, their cost, efficiency and
innovation disadvantages lead to crisis and probable
collapse. Major examples of this process occurred

following the collapse of the Soviet Union and its associated regimes in central and eastern Europe. A central problem with protection is that there is rarely a neutral arbiter who can determine when a genuine case for protection no longer applies; while there are plenty of special interests able to insist that it should continue. This does not dispose of the genuine arguments around infant industries and races to the bottom; but advocates of protection on social grounds need to avoid being naïve about the political realities of governments and corporations exploiting them. Free trade enables firms and national economies to specialise in what they do best, keeps everyone under competitive pressure to improve, and enables poor countries to join in the world economy, gradually pulling their people out of poverty – something from which they are excluded if rich countries protect their industries from competition.

Facilitating links among people

Closely linked to debates over free trade are those around national, racial and similar boundaries. Neoliberals do not care about the quality of human relationships in themselves, as these are externalities to the market. However, one consequence of the triumph of neoliberal over statist approaches to economic questions has been to open borders, facilitating the movement of people, ideas and cultural practices.

With the partial exception of the EU, state action usually means actions by nation states. Left to themselves, these define an insider population and protect and enhance national characteristics, either in isolation from or sometimes in hostility to those of other nations. Periods of particularly strong national economic protectionism have also been those of powerful nationalism, occasionally overlapping into open conflict. A major example was the period between the First and Second World Wars. The only internationalism that flourishes in periods of strong national rivalry is imperialism, as in the decades running up to the First World War when the states of Europe, led by the British, colonised other regions of the world. There was as a result considerable cultural interchange, but always on terms of the domination of many different peoples by those of one core nation. The tensions set up by this situation exploded in the late 19th and 20th centuries in demands for national liberation, which in turn unleashed its own nationalisms.

Neoliberal economic strategies weaken the hold of the state, and therefore reduce divisions among people and restrictions on their movements that are imposed by states. Many citizens support these divisions, because they share the suspicions about people from other places that centuries of nationalism have encouraged; but others appreciate the opportunities for extending their lives that neoliberal internationalism brings. This does not mean that neoliberals cannot be nationalists; they might draw the line at free markets in goods and services, but discourage exchanges among people themselves. But there are tensions in such an approach, as it is difficult in practice to maintain such distinctions.

Markets do not acknowledge differences of nationality, race or gender, so market neoliberalism is difficult to fit into a nationalist mould. Similar points apply to corporate neoliberalism. Many transnational corporations do not respect national differences in their own practices. They recruit staff at all levels internationally, producing mixed work teams.

This transcendence of national differences and facilitation of cross-national mixing of people by neoliberalism is an externality. I have here regarded it as a positive one, but readers with a strong belief in national identity and separateness may well prefer to locate this theme in the previous section of this discussion, as something that is 'wrong' with neoliberalism, a negative externality. Assessment depends on the reader's point of view.

Conclusion: Neoliberalism's virtues

Neoliberalism has no monopoly over these valuable aspects of its legacy. Neoclassical economic theory (which is an analytical technique, not a political doctrine) can teach us about opportunity costs and the value of efficient allocation of funds. Much political theory warns us against over-estimating democracy's capacity to equate the interests of governments and governed. Free trade was practised rigorously by the Nordic countries during their long decades of political dominance by social democracy. Liberals, social democrats and moderate conservatives have all encouraged the free movement of people. However, neoliberal dominance has been the spur to the spread of each of them around many parts of the world in recent years. And there is a risk that some of them would be undermined in the course of any general rollback of neoliberalism's achievements.

Chapter 3

CAN NEOLIBERALISM BE
REFORMED?

While governments inspired by neoliberalism make compromises with public spending and regulation all the time, they do so solely as a reluctant recognition of pressing, hopefully temporary, political realities; their default preferred position is always to make government as small as possible, apart perhaps from its defence and security activities. In 2014 the Conservative government in the UK announced its determination to return to the public spending levels of the 1930s – that is, before the construction of the modern welfare state. In the US, the Trump administration has already begun to unravel the regulation of the banking sector that had been put in place following 2008 to try to prevent a recurrence of the financial crisis. In several countries, banks that in the wake of the crisis had trumpeted their conversion to the pursuit of less hectic short-term trading have returned to their pre-2007 ways of doing business.

Readiness of neoliberals to accept a need to reform their model rather than just make occasional temporary concessions would have to result from a perception that the model itself was embarked on a self-destructive path. That however assumes the existence of persons and institutions in a position to take strategic action on the basis of such a perception. For market neoliberal thinkers, like Hayek, the beauty of the pure market was precisely that no one was in a position to take strategic action: life would be guided by the mass of tiny individual acts of sale and purchase. Market neoliberals have no answer to major malfunctions of the model itself. The position of corporate neoliberalism is rather different; some corporations and very wealthy groups are capable of either taking strategic action themselves or of urging governments to do so. Therefore the first question that needs to be addressed in assessing neoliberalism's capacity for reform is: who would be the strategic actors in such reform? We can then go on to address two key areas where such actors might in principle be motivated to take action: the threat posed to capitalist economies by growing inequality; and the challenge to neoliberalism of xenophobic nationalism.

Corporate neoliberalism's strategic actors

In *The Communist Manifesto* (1848) Karl Marx and Friedrich Engels asserted that 'the executive of the modern state is but a committee for managing the common affairs of the bourgeoisie'. It was intended as a criticism of the limited social responsibility of governments in 19th century capitalism. A sharper criticism might be made against early 21st century capitalism: it is losing the capacity even to have a committee to manage its common affairs. The mid-20th century German *Ordoliberalen* saw government as essential in setting and subsequently maintaining a perfectly competitive order; it was then necessary to ensure that governments did not do much else. Over subsequent decades intellectual leadership of the neoliberal project passed to US economists who have viewed the state as inherently incompetent, and have therefore wanted to limit its role even further. Their vision has been impossible to realise in practice, but their intellectual success means that contemporary neoliberals are in difficulties when confronted by needs for action that go beyond the market's own capacities. The major differences here between market and corporate neoliberals can be explored by considering the different answers given by both to two sets of questions:

- Does emphasising the importance of the market mean that as many aspects of human life as possible should be brought within its scope? If so, what kind of power has to be wielded to force life into such a mode? If not, how are parts of life that remain outside the market to be protected from it?
- Is neoliberalism compatible with the pursuit of long-term goals? Can its institutions protect the long-term from the short-term?

The market or nothing but the market?

The *Ordoliberalen* were very clear that major areas of life had to be protected from the market, though they insisted that within the economy as such it had to reign supreme. Their formative years having taken place during the final crisis of the Weimar Republic, its struggles between communists and others, and the eventual triumph of the Hitler regime, they hoped for a world where community life, religion and leisure pursuits could be beyond the reach of both economics and politics. As Bonefeld has made clear, this was what they meant by the 'social' market – not, as the term is used nowadays, to refer to a market softened by a welfare state. Once again, as leadership of neoliberal thinking passed to US economists and as economic theory became more sophisticated, this stance changed radically. Neoliberals increasingly sought means of extending the reach of the market, applying market concepts to penetrate institutions like the family. Organisations in most areas of life (for example, churches, cultural bodies) have been persuaded by neoliberal governments and sponsors to structure themselves as though they were profit-making concerns. Young people have been encouraged to value education mainly in terms of the income it might bring; and there are many other examples.

The original *ordoliberal* vision of major parts of life being sustained outside the market but also without state support remains attractive to some neoliberals. A recent British example was the policy of a Conservative prime minister, David Cameron, to encourage a 'big society'. This referred to the mass of voluntary organisations that perform tasks that would otherwise fall on public social services and require government finance; releasing the energies of the big society would therefore reduce the need for public spending and consequently public employment. Unpaid volunteers would replace public service workers. Following an initial high-profile launch, the strategy quickly evaporated. Cameron's New Labour predecessor, Tony Blair, had a similar vision, when he announced that his 'Third Way' political movement had natural affinities with the 'third sector', the name given in the UK to the voluntary sector, outside both market and state. Little came of it.

While societies are certainly made richer and more attractive when citizens are engaged in a large number of activities to help each other, there are major difficulties if governments seek to encourage them as part of a strategy to reduce their own spending and activities. *Ordoliberalen* would have been suspicious of government becoming at all involved in society in this way, as they would have feared that it would be unable to resist the temptation to seek to control voluntary activities. This is indeed what happens, especially when governments' main motive is to use volunteers to do work that would otherwise fall on the state. This demotivates volunteers, as they observe not only that the state is turning them into its agents rather than allowing them to develop their own priorities, but that their action is being used by government as a reason to reduce its own activities, leading to no net increase in the services provided.

Another form taken by voluntary action is philanthropy: the use of private wealth to fund activities outside the market and without a profit motive. A wide range of activities from social need to high culture and scientific research are funded in this way, enabling these to thrive in a manner that would not be possible under strict market rules, activities on which neoliberal governments do not want to spend money. However, so attractive are these possibilities that governments do indirectly share in the financing of philanthropic activities. They do this by offering not to tax individual and corporate income that is used for nominated philanthropic purposes. This certainly releases funds for activities that might otherwise be neglected, but it comes at a price. If government offers tax rebates, it has less available itself to spend. This serves the neoliberal preference for low taxes, but it means in effect delegating public policy-making to very rich people, who are able to direct a proportion of public spending to projects that they rather than any political processes have chosen. Not only do the rich become ever richer, and not only does the reach of their wealth keep extending as more things are brought within the market, but they also have a large say in how residual public spending is used.

Outside the philanthropic activities of the very rich, most voluntary activities take the form of a mass of actions by ordinary individuals, who have to find funds in order to keep going. Set beside the giants of corporate wealth and the state, these are tiny, and constantly struggling to make ends meet. They increasingly have to appeal to corporations and the rich for financial help, which means that the voluntary activities that secure most support are those that do things of which the wealthy approve.

Similar points apply to the practice of corporate social responsibility (CSR), where firms accept responsibility for the negative externalities that their activities produce. For example, they may choose to abide by certain environmental standards or avoid various forms of labour exploitation. Less frequently, banks might abjure irresponsible trading practices. In principle these activities will make a firm less profitable, though their protagonists have various arguments that suggest that this may be untrue. There may be reputational gains from pursuing ethical practices, and the kind of innovation often associated with that pursuit might also characterise a corporation as more generally innovative; socially responsible firms are usually high value-added ones. But corporate responsibility shares the problem of other forms of voluntary action, that decisions as to which responsibilities to acknowledge (and which to ignore) are taken by a very small number of corporate leaders and wealthy individuals. Despite these limitations, CSR can help deal with some negative externalities.

For extreme market neoliberals, all these social market activities are problematic. If the market represents the peak of human rationality and the perfection of individual choice, then no institution should stand outside it,

as all would have their efficiency improved by partaking
in it. From this perspective the voluntary sector is just as
unattractive as the public one. This should in theory be
as true of relations between children and parents, or
sexual partners, or among friends, as those between the
buyers and sellers of fruit and vegetables. An initial
problem faced by advocates of this view is that many of
these institutions have long existed outside the reach of
the market. To bring them into it would require government action to prevent access to the resource in question
that does not take a market form. This has certainly
been done in the past; the privatisation of much
common land in the 18th century was a major example.
The shareholder value maximisation form of corporate
governance is a still current instance. This reform has
been part of neoliberals' attempts at reducing the role
of powerful senior executives, who were seen as having
interests separate from those of shareholders. It therefore constitutes a victory of the market form over the
corporate version of neoliberalism. Linked to it is the
current practice of having a large part of senior executives' remuneration take the form of profit-related
bonuses, tying them into shareholders' interests, and
accounting for a good deal in the extraordinary rise in
executives' remuneration in recent years. Originating in
American and British corporate law, shareholder value
maximisation has been imitated in many other countries, creating problems for their former practices. For
example, it threatens the German concept that a firm
has responsibilities to its workforce and local community
as well as to shareholders.

Its effectiveness as a means of asserting shareholder rule has been weakened, partly because many shareholders are themselves large organisations closer to corporate than to market neoliberalism, and partly for the opposite reason that much share trading is carried out by computers, where a shareholder might hold a firm's assets for a brief period of time, with no human being actually knowing that the asset was held. On the other hand, it has helped produce the high level of mergers and acquisitions typical of contemporary capitalism, where firms that fail to maximise profits are rapidly vulnerable to takeover. Ironically, this has led only to reduced competition in some sectors and has therefore strengthened corporate over market neoliberalism. We shall return to some further problems raised by this when we consider the issue of short-termism.

One type of capitalist organisation that has been harmed by the shareholder maximisation model is that known as the 'mutual'. This is where a firm is owned by its members rather than by shareholders, all profits being invested back into the enterprise to improve members' benefits. It is a form taken by many pension, insurance and housing organisations, the last in the form of building societies. It operates fully within the capitalist market economy, but does not follow the neoliberal rule of shareholder maximisation. Neoliberal governments have therefore encouraged mutuals to turn themselves into profit-maximising companies. At the very time that British New Labour governments were celebrating a third sector, they were encouraging the transformation of the building societies from mutuals into profit-maximising banks. Some of those that did so were at the heart of the collapse of British banks that was among the triggers of the 2007-8 crisis.

Strict market neoliberals are more likely to insist on rigorous conformity to market rule than corporate neoliberals, who advocate corporate leaders taking political and social initiatives outside the strict frame of a firm's market activities. Only corporate, not market, neoliberalism therefore provides potential strategic actors in the form of corporate 'statesmen' capable of perceiving general problems and challenges for the system as a whole – as is the case with some prominent business exponents of CSR. In general we have in these pages identified corporate neoliberalism as a rather corrupted form that loses the characteristics of pure competition that are among the attractions of the market, and as making possible the dubious lobbying links between corporations and governments, anathema to market neoliberals and left-wing critics alike. Is this the nearest we can get today to a committee for managing the common affairs of the bourgeoisie? An instructive example of this confusion in neoliberalism is the on-going history of food safety regulation in the UK. Until 2011 the country had a standard bureaucratic and scientific approach to this. Committees dominated by food scientists would prepare rules for safety standards in the cultivation, manufacture and sale of food products; and the regulations were enforced by local government. For pure neoliberals this is unacceptable; food standards should be left to the market and the rule of *caveat emptor* (let the buyer beware). But this is politically impossible given the difficulty consumers have in knowing what happens in the food chain. Faced with this problem but insistent on dismantling the public regulation system, the neoliberal Conservative and Liberal Democratic coalition government embarked on a course of reducing the scale of the Food Standards Authority's work, diluting its scientific membership with representatives of the food industry; and weakening local authority inspection capacity, privatising much of it and promising light-touch regulation to the main food companies. In this highly incoherent way, corporate neoliberalism emerged as a compromise between public regulation and market neoliberalism.

Under neoliberalism governments have lost confidence that they are competent to play much of a strategic role themselves; do the corporate leaders and wealthy individuals who have access to them have any incentives to persuade them to work for some general interests rather than just pressing their own concerns? But this represents a major compromise for the idea of market dominance, and becomes a key question as neoliberalism faces major problems of its own viability. The extreme goal of bringing virtually all human life into market exchanges is impossible to realise. But, given the enormous dominance of the market in a society that has been reformed by neoliberals, what protects the viability of those areas of life that remain outside it, especially once neoliberals have also succeeded in residualising the role of government? The mechanisms that some neolib-erals offer – volunteers, philanthropy, CSR – seem either puny or to compromise the market neoliberal ideal.

Neoliberalism and the long term

A fundamental attraction for neoliberals of the market is that it avoids the need for long-term planning – an activity that they see, not without reason, as belonging to a powerful central state, which is almost certain to get things wrong, as it cannot anticipate innovation and therefore tends to inhibit it. The neoliberal long term emerges from the mass of tiny, individual, short-term transactions that constitute the market. If we can assume that actors are rational, they would be able to see when an accumulation of such transactions was leading in a less profitable direction, and would adjust accordingly. (For example, if investment in stocks in technology companies shows signs of excessive optimism about long-term prospects, wise investors will start selling shares in them, and the market will eventually normalise.)

In this vision shareholders are investors who rationally consider the substantive prospects of the stocks they purchase, though externalities as well as public goods that cannot be included in firms' decisions are ignored. Let us now make some different assumptions. Assume that investors purchase stocks purely with the intention of packaging them with others and selling them on as quickly as possible, and in some cases the investors are computers. Firms that fail to make a quick profit, because they are investing in long-term projects, will see their share prices fall and will be vulnerable to takeovers by firms promising to deliver higher dividends by dropping long-term projects. Under these circumstances the accumulation of masses of individual transactions is unable to produce a satisfactory long term. It certainly cannot do anything about problems of environmental damage and climate change.

Following the neoliberal deregulation of financial markets that occurred in the 1980s, first in the UK and US but later across the world, that latter model became increasingly the realistic one. Deregulation led to an explosion of new ideas for risk sharing through secondary and derivatives markets. It became possible to leverage loans on very little collateral, and the number of participants in the markets was growing as deregulation spread across the world. Traders could buy private and public debt and sell it on in parcels to other investors, with larger numbers of players involved at each stage. The share of any one risk borne by an individual investor or bank became smaller at each new iteration. It seemed that scarcity had been abolished, and that the rules of classical economics no longer operated. The market had floated free from itself. Operators in these markets had little incentive to check the exact nature of the risk in any bundle of debt they were purchasing, as they intended to sell it on very rapidly to a large number of other purchasers; the market's need for fully informed participants was not met but was felt to be unnecessary in this constantly expanding financial universe. A flaw in the system was that, although any one bank's holdings of one particular risky debt was small and in their hands for only a short period, at any one moment they were all holding very large numbers of these small shares. Sooner or later a doubt over some debts was bound to lead to a loss of confidence in some banks. When this happened, trust in banks' integrity spread rapidly across the system, creating the chaos that was the 2007-8 crisis.

Many critics have argued that it was bankers' greed and irresponsibility that caused the problem, and that the solution lies in higher standards of corporate ethics. This is however extremely difficult to do within a free market. As Chuck Prince, the CEO of Citigroup bank famously remarked in an interview with the *Financial Times* in July 2007, on the eve of the crisis: 'As long as the music is playing, you've got to get up and dance'. Any firms that had withdrawn from the trading frenzy while it lasted would have become less profitable than their rivals who continued indulging in risky trades; their share values would have fallen; and they would have been vulnerable to takeover by other banks willing to act irresponsibly. In several cases the dance lured many of the world's leading banks from insouciant irresponsibility into serious criminality, as the subsequent mass of legal cases and fines have demonstrated. Far from being self-correcting, the market's incentives made everything worse. There was, in sum, a major collective action problem: everyone stood to gain from some regulation of behaviour, but the market excluded any participants within the system from taking steps to end what was going on. Governments and central banks, acting in concert across the world, had to intervene, initially to stem the crisis and afterwards to reconstruct a new regulatory framework.

Technically, there are no difficulties in designing such frameworks. The Basel Committee on Banking Supervision (BCBS) – an international committee of central banks and banking supervision authorities - is seeking to toughen the rules on banks' capital adequacy ratios (the relationship between a bank's assets and the speculative trades it conducts). But the BCBS lacks international statutory powers, and in any case tends to stay as close as it can to the neoliberal rule that the markets know better than public authorities. It uses measures of risk developed by banks themselves and by the private credit ratings agencies that were among those responsible for failing to appreciate the extent of banks' problems in 2007. During the period of the Obama administration in the US there had been an attempt to get tougher. The Dodd-Frank Act of 2010 raised capital holdings requirements on banks and regulated their risky investment activities. However, early in the life of the Trump administration (June 2017) Congress voted to weaken many of Dodd-Frank's provisions. Very few bankers involved in recent criminal scandals have been imprisoned: 'too big to jail', as some observers have commented.

Neoliberals argue that these post-2008 attempts to rein in bank irresponsibility serve only to hamper trading, making it more difficult to share risk, and therefore hinder innovative activity. They might also point out that types of investor who manage to stand outside the short-term share price model, such as venture capitalists, depend on an ability to keep some funds in volatile markets in order to have the resources for longer-term projects. But these advantages have to be set against the overall loss in welfare that occurs when an unregulated system collapses, as it did in 2008. Market neoliberals also claim, with considerable justification, that the expectation that corporate neoliberal governments would bail banks out – that they were 'too big to fail' – encouraged them to take irresponsible risks, and that the post-2008 bail-outs will only give banks incentives to take even bigger risks in future. But here too one has to set the damage done by bailouts against the danger of a total collapse of the global economy had nothing been done to stem the haemorrhage of share values that was taking place. Calculations must be made of the trade-off between the gains and losses from deregulation, but although neoliberals talk the language of calculation and opportunity costs, in practice they always make the *a priori* assumption that costs of regulation and public intervention outweigh any benefits.

The situation is one commonly met in game theory: where there is short-term competitive gain from dangerous behaviour but long-term loss, it is rational to seek external regulation to protect oneself from one's own behaviour. The example usually given concerns participants in dangerous sports. (For a good discussion, see Robert Frank's *The Darwin Economy*.) If individuals are given a free choice whether to wear protective equipment that will protect them from serious injury, but which will impede their performance against competitors who do not wear the equipment, the great majority of players will abjure the protection. But the same players will, completely rationally, support the general imposition of a rule that everyone must wear it.

The market itself cannot enable its participants to make choices of this kind, but large corporations and associations of firms have a degree of autonomy from the short-term pressures of the market, which should enable them to act strategically. Large banks, fearing another crash, but unable to miss profit-making opportunities if they arise, should support regulation designed to prevent the situation getting out of control again. As with the discussion of 'the market or nothing but the market?', corporate neoliberalism might paradoxically hold out a better prospect of responsible business behaviour than the market form.

The evidence on whether or not they do this is mixed. The weakness of plans to improve the BSBS Basel agreement suggests that banks' immediate interests carry considerable weight with regulators. Plans for a financial transactions tax (designed to reduce extreme velocity of financial transactions) by the EU have been watered down following intensive lobbying by the financial sector. (For a detailed account, see Lisa Kastner's 2017 study.)

There has been a different experience with the submission of banks to statutory 'stress tests'. Central bank officials test the ability of banks to be able to confront a range of shocks. If they fail the tests, they can be required to change their capitalisation base or seek a merger with another bank. Such tests have been required by the European Central Bank, the US Federal Reserve Bank, and the Bank of England. They are compatible with moderate neoliberalism, as they amount to a shadow testing of market pressures, but they are unwelcome to extreme neoliberals, as they involve public authorities intervening rather than allowing market forces to work by themselves. Banks in general seem to have welcomed them, as they protect the system from risky banks. A collapse of banks' confidence in each other had been a major aspect of the immediate aftermath of the crisis.

The restoration of trust has also been a major feature of the European Central Bank's financial compensation scheme (a similar measure has been introduced by the Bank of England). This scheme is designed to restore the confidence in financial institutions of small savers. Banks are required to contribute an insurance scheme, which compensates investors in financial firms up to a maximum of €100,000. Institutions do not oppose the scheme and contribute to the funds, because they know that, in the absence of something of this kind, in the wake of the crisis they would have difficulty persuading small wealth holders to part with their money. This is a further example of a reform to the neoliberal model that seems to require state (i.e. central bank) initiative and therefore external regulation, but which tends to the preservation of the market economy.

These differences in the finance industry's responses to various post-crisis initiatives show what might be expected: where a public policy provides financial firms with assurances that help themselves, it is welcomed; where it seeks to restrain their risk-taking, they oppose it, even though they might seem to have a long-term interest in such measures. The problem is that *neither banks nor governments have a strong interest in the long term.* Banks wanted to get back to making very large profits out of high-risk activity; if they can make enough money in a short period, they can probably sit back on their piles of wealth when the next crash comes. Also, since the sector as a whole and certain banks within it, are essential to the functioning of the system, public authorities will have to bail them out at public expense if they fail, as happened after 2008. For their part, governments have been desperate for banks to get back to being profitable as soon as possible, so that the bailouts can end. The quickest route to that has been through tolerating a return to high-risk lending.

As in the previous discussion of the extent of the role of the market in society, we confront a tension between the market and corporate forms of neoliberalism. To the extent that the former dominates, we have a system that imposes certain kinds of responsible behaviour – profits can be made only by providing goods and services that consumers want at prices they can afford – but which is incapable of producing measures that will safeguard longer-term interests that cannot be achieved within the market itself. To the extent that corporate neoliberalism dominates, corporations may sometimes have an incentive to deal with externalities, to support causes that cannot be helped by the market, and assist the pursuit of long-term concerns. But they do this without any systematic market or regulatory constraints on pursuit of their selfish concerns. This incoherence within neoliberalism may serve to strengthen it rather than tear it apart. Given that there are no rules guaranteeing the dominance of either form, and that the difference is barely recognised, the system can shift and adjust, and probably ensure its survival. But capacity for strategic action remains weak. We shall explore this in relation to the two issues of rising inequality and xenophobia.

Inequality and mass consumption

One consequence of governments engaging in a race to the bottom over taxation has been to shift an increasing share of taxation away from corporations and the rich on to lower and medium earners. For neoliberals of all kinds this has been a great achievement: the wealthy, whose interests they are mainly concerned to protect, are able to become richer, while taxes (and therefore public spending) are under pressures for reduction as the mass of voters resent their growing burden. But this resentment together with growing inequality is presenting certain major risks to the neoliberal model.

Partly for these fiscal reasons, partly because of other factors, the rewards of wealth (including the salaries of very highly paid executives) are already growing far more rapidly than the incomes of the rest of the population, as Thomas Piketty has shown in *Capital in the 21ˢᵗ Century*. Politically this change further favours neoliberalism, as the political power of wealth can be deployed to ensure that high incomes are taxed lightly and that business regulation is relaxed to help the interests of wealth holders. Michael Förster and his colleagues at the Organization for Economic Cooperation and Development (OECD) have calculated that in the USA the top 1% of income earners took 47% of total economic growth between 1979 and 2007. In the UK the figure was 26%. The OECD had access to similar data for only a few other (European) countries, but these suggest a lower figure, from 4 to 11%. The US and the UK are the two countries where neoliberal ideas developed and affected public policy with least restraint, but there is considerable evidence that similar policies have been spreading. What has happened in those two countries over the past 30 years should therefore be expected to be imitated elsewhere.

The OECD has probed the reasons for these increases in inequality in western countries. It found that large rises in incomes have been concentrated among senior managers and some professionals, particularly in the

financial sector. Very high earners are likely to have their
income source divided between salaries and investment
earnings to a far greater extent than is the case of the
rest of the workforce. The 'bottom' 90% have between
70 and 85% of their incomes in the form of wages and
salaries; the top 0.01% in contrast have only 40% in this
form. There have been strong trends in many countries
for taxes on investment earnings to be reduced far more
than those on wages and salaries. Between 1981 and
2010 taxation rates on the highest incomes across the
OECD area declined from 66 to 42%; corporate as
opposed to individual income tax has dropped from 47
to 25%; taxes on dividends from 75 to 42%. These
numbers relate to taxation rates, and do not take
account of any increases that might have taken place in
the ability of wealthy people to avoid tax, though the
deregulation of global finance that took place during the
period has made legal tax avoidance easier.

Although inequality was rising in this way, and real
incomes for ordinary workers had been static,
consumers in the US and elsewhere were able to sustain
their consumption. This was made possible by a considerable rise in both public and private debt, financed in
turn by a growth of financial markets made possible by
the global deregulation that was one of neoliberalism's
main achievements. Eventually the instability of this
growth helped produce the crisis of 2007-08. It is for
this reason that the IMF and OECD have become
concerned at the rise in income inequality (see in particular the OECD's 2015 report *In It Together: Why Less*

Inequality Benefits All). They fear the consequences for future economic growth if the wealthy absorb too much of its proceeds, leaving middle-income households dependent on risky credit to sustain their standard of living, and discouraging lower-income families from taking up educational opportunities.

In *Buying Time* and in *How Will Capitalism End?* Wolfgang Streeck has argued that the indebtedness trap could threaten the model of capitalism to which we have become accustomed, one dependent on mass consumption. This is not the only historical form that capitalism has taken. Until the mid-20th century the mass of the population could afford only basic products: food, some clothes, a few sticks of furniture. Capitalists depended for opportunities to innovate and produce up-market goods on very small, but high-spending, numbers of aristocratic and bourgeois purchasers of luxury goods. One reason why pre-democratic elites resisted so strongly the demands of the growing industrial working class was that they could not see how such an economy could produce enough wealth to raise general living standards. Two major historical developments made possible mass consumption capitalism. First came mass production in the US motor industry in the early 20th century; second was Keynesian demand management in the Scandinavian, then the British and American economies either side of the Second World War. Together they helped create a mass population with money in their pockets. From that point the extraordinary rise in the consumption of goods and later services launched the unprecedented rise in prosperity that we have inherited and largely take for granted.

This has also been the period in which, as Piketty has shown, wealth and income became far less unequally distributed than at any time since the 18th century (which is as far back as records, mainly in France, the UK and the US) go. But Piketty then plots a resurgence of inequality since the late 1970s, the period of growing neoliberal dominance. Can capitalism based on mass consumption survive a period of intensified inequality without continued use of unsustainable debt among middle- and lower-income households? The question will become more pressing if, as some predict, digitalisation threatens employment in a wide range of middle- and even higher-income occupations. Of course, globalisation will be bringing new mass consumers among the vast populations of the rapidly industrialising populations of the Far East. Should we envisage a future in which the populations of the existing advanced economies become unimportant to global capitalism as either workers or consumers? Would their societies be able to remain even residually democratic under such circumstances? How would these 'redundant' populations react to their growing marginalisation? Do governments have the power to offset these changes, at least through fiscal policy? Would governments that increased tax burdens on capital or financial transactions find that firms left their borders for jurisdictions that did not do so? This is their principal fear. In a globalised economy it is not adequate for national governments even to be only committees for managing the common affairs of the bourgeoisie if they can manage those affairs only at a national level. The OECD and IMF – initially among the main institutions pressing adoption of neoliberal policies - have international competence and their staffs have already perceived the long-term dangers to global capitalism. In addition to arguing that the growth of inequality is damaging economies, they have criticised the Basel reforms for staying too close to banks' interests (see OECD research paper by P. Slovik); and they have wondered whether neoliberalism has been 'oversold' (see IMF contribution from Jonathan Ostry and colleagues). In *International Regulatory Co-operation* the OECD has encouraged transnational regulatory co-operation as an essential step to gaining some purchase over global economic behaviour. But these bodies lack executive power, which they can derive only from their member governments. The future of democratic capitalism may well depend on major global corporations and super-rich individuals listening to these international bodies and being willing to allow governments to restrain the inequalities from which they have themselves gained so much profit.

Neoliberalism and xenophobia

We are already beginning to see one of the possible answers to the question of how redundant populations react to marginalisation. The process has begun around the peripheries of many, even most, advanced economies, where people are showing an anger that seems to have been ignited from the slow fuse of the financial crisis. It takes the form of xenophobic, anti-globalisation movements and parties. An important part of the rhetoric of these movements is to attack neoliberal elites, who, they claim, have damaged the lives of many people in the advanced world. Globalisation and deregulation, it is argued, have been used to export jobs away from the advanced world to developing countries; and immigration has been encouraged to put pressure on the wages and working conditions of native workers. To date, xenophobic movements are challenging neoliberalism more effectively than social democrats or greens have done. Should we therefore expect corporations to respond by accepting some regulation of their activities and some additional corporate taxation, in order to ward off this challenge and restore confidence in the globalisation project? Or do alliances with xenophobic movements enable neoliberals to achieve one of their main aims: to keep democratic politics at levels where it cannot reach the activities of major corporations – i.e. at the level of the nation state? Do neoliberals see the rise of xenophobia and nationalism as the source of allies against their critics or as a potentially fatal blow to their own project?

The debate in the UK over the country leaving the EU (so-called 'Brexit') illustrates the ambiguities of the business position. Most large British firms, as well as their key representative bodies (the Confederation of British Industry, the Institute of Directors, the Engineering Employers Federation and the National Union of Farmers) and the main media voices of the British business community (the *Financial Times* and *The Economist*) strongly supported the UK remaining in the EU. Despite its regulatory role in relation to business interests, it is seen as a business-friendly institution that promotes free trade. However, with the exception of the *Financial Times* and *The Economist*, they did not campaign very strongly in public for the Remain side. Perhaps they feared that their advocacy would strengthen populist opposition; perhaps they did not want to intervene strongly in an issue where their preferred political party, the Conservatives, was heavily divided. Meanwhile, hedge funds, that part of the financial sector, the highly short-term nature of whose activities causes particular instability in markets, and that therefore thrives on an absence of regulation, heavily supported the campaign to leave the EU with their massive funds. Far less importantly, small firms not engaged in exports and imports tended to be hostile to the EU as a source of regulations that they believed, rightly or wrongly, would not have developed under a purely national regulatory regime.

It would be possible for business interests to take a more cynically strategic view. In the UK a primarily xenophobic opposition to the EU could serve two business purposes. First, by taking the heat off banks and other financial institutions for blame for the 2008 crisis, Brexit could prove a valuable diversionary tactic. There is certainly evidence that an important element in the promotion of Donald Trump's campaign to become president of the US came from billionaires worried about eventually being blamed for 2008, and seeing Trump's invective against Mexicans and Moslems as providing useful alternative targets for rage. Immigrants, refugees and the EU provide safer targets for rage than the banks whose actions had actually caused the crisis. Many people, probably a majority, would fear the threat to their living standards and overall social stability if there were to be major political challenges to the power of big capital, on which they depend for their livelihoods. Second, if - as the Brexit campaign maintains - democracy should remain fixed at the level of the nation state and go no higher, then democracy and public regulation can never meet capitalism at the global level where it operates. Global business; national politics - that makes a useful slogan for evading an effective regulation that in an international economy. If such a hamstringing of politics and democracy can be presented as regaining sovereignty and taking back control, then so much the better.

However, flirtation with xenophobia is a dangerous game for neoliberals to play. The anti-global turn could begin to interfere with free trade, as the Trump administration clearly threatens to do. Stirring up popular rage can get out of control. Not surprisingly therefore, we find major divisions among capitalist interests. To the extent that those who are worried about instability dominate, important policy compromises can be done between neoliberals and social democrats, greens, social liberals and others who actively seek a regulated market order. To the extent that those seeking to make use of xenophobia dominate, the more dangerous is the world likely to become. There will be no progress on such issues as climate change and global labour exploitation, and continued low-level encouragement of ethnic and other cultural tensions. Given that crises of different kinds are producing major shocks in predominately Islamic parts of the world, producing flows of refugees and isolated acts of terrorism, the prospects for a secure world are bleak. These events impact further on opinion in the advanced countries, encouraging further inter-cultural hostility and widespread desires to close countries off from contact with the outside world.

Conclusion

This discussion of how neoliberal governments and corporations are likely to confront the dilemmas facing their project has revealed major problems for both neoliberalism itself and for its relations with the rest of society. Is the market the form of social organisation that all aspects of life should seek to join, or should some areas of life be kept free from it? If the former, through what means is extension of the market to be enforced? If the latter, what protects those areas of life that remain outside the overwhelmingly dominant market order? Is it acceptable if part of the answer is the good will of wealthy individuals and large corporations?

The market is unable to be self-correcting and take care of the long term, given the global nature of such issues as climate change and over-sophisticated financial

markets. This does not mean that we should turn back
to the idea of an all-knowing planning state, but it does
mean that we need institutions capable of responding to
major issues of externalities and public goods. These
will necessarily mainly be governments. What role is it
acceptable for corporations and business associations to
have alongside them? They are capable of strategic
thinking in a way inhibited by the pure market; but they
are lobbies for their own interests. The fundamental
antagonism between market and corporate neoliberalism rarely surfaces in open conflict, but it confronts the
whole project with dilemmas that it is hard to resolve.
On both the issue of the extent of the market and the
capacity for long-term action, market neoliberals have a
stance that is theoretically pure but far from the reality
of the modern economy, while corporate neoliberals are
far more practical but occupy a stance that is impossible
to defend and possibly corrupt. The only development
likely to make either of them accept something beyond
tactical compromises is the threat to their dominance
posed by xenophobic populism, but here neoliberal
politicians and business people are cross-pressured by
the temptation to use resurgent nationalism to push the
powers of states into complete weakness.

Disputes over the governance of capitalism usually set
free markets against the state. Advocates of the former
stress the rights of individuals to choose; supporters of
the latter point to shared, collective interests that cannot
be achieved through a series of individual choices. But
the reality of the situation shows both sides in a poor

light. Many markets are dominated by small numbers of corporations who do not so much respond to customers' demands as shape those demands through marketing strategies so that they suit what firms want to produce. On the other hand, not only is the state prey to takeover by politicians keen to advance their own careers and (sometimes) private wealth, but more immediately relevant to the present study, in a global world national states cannot truly represent general public interests.

Certainly states represent a *collective* interest, as do local governments. In that capacity they can do highly important work, representing the public concerns of their citizens. However, the claim that the nation state represents a universality, a limitless general interest rather than just the collective interests of a defined territorial group becomes highly questionable the more that national boundaries cannot contain the consequences of actions carried out within those boundaries. This has always been true; in particular the European colonial powers secured economic advantages for their ruling groups and mass populations through military conquest and the robbery of resources. Today we are more sensitive about issues of this kind, but governments as much as firms and markets are major players at dumping negative externalities on other parts of the world, particularly of course environmental damage. Our high standard of living is partly boosted by the availability of very cheap imports from countries where workers have virtually no rights at all. Only transnational governance can tackle issues of this kind. This is not an impossible dream;

institutions capable of performing this kind of role exist: the EU, the OECD, the IMF, the World Bank, the World Trade Organisation, the International Labour Organisation. Mechanisms for extending their governance activities further are conceivable, and there is evidence that the staffs within these organisations have a grasp of many of the issues involved. They are also becoming awareness of the disillusion with globalisation that is fuelling destabilising xenophobic movements. As transnational bodies, these organisations are themselves likely to become the targets of these sentiments.

But transnational regimes could develop a power to counter the power of business only if they were supported by democratic energy. This is extremely difficult to achieve under any circumstances, most popular mobilisation being heavily based on the nation state. Current xenophobic trends are intensifying this, as they *prevent* the development of popular political energy above that level. Transnational popular mobilisations do exist. Organisations like Amnesty International, Médécins sans Frontières, Oxfam, Greenpeace, Transparency International manage to organise actions across national boundaries in ways that nationally rooted political parties find difficult. So does a growing range of more militant but also more transitory protest groups like those around most inter-governmental meetings like the G20. These all help to develop that elusive entity, an international framework of citizens' actions. They contribute to the liberalism and pluralism of the international realm, in that they set a flexible, open discussion-based set of actions alongside and against the rigid secrecy of the discussions that go on among governments and between them and large corporations. But they are hardly democratic; the number and range of people engaged is tiny and they lack a formal democratic mandate.

Unfamiliar political confrontations are developing as neoliberalism runs into crises and blockages. Campaigns of popular mobilisation against capitalism's excesses find their best but unlikely dialogue partners among the increasingly concerned technocrats in the international organisations. These people confront an increasingly anti-liberal form of democracy and anti-humanitarian populism. Neoliberalism, already in confusion between the lack of realism of its pure market form and the incoherence of its corporate form, stands between the two. It can be reformed only if and when the world's major capitalist interests come to see that flirtation with xenophobic forces threatens their own longer-term interests; and that their own short-term actions compromise their own long-term needs; and if and when democratic politics can reach effectively beyond the level of the nation state.

WORKS CITED IN THE TEXT

Bonefeld, W. 2017. *The Strong State and the Free Economy.* London: Rowan and Littlefield.

Cahill, D. and Konings, M. 2017. *Neoliberalism.* Cambridge: Polity.

Crouch, C. 2011. *The Strange Non-Death of Neoliberalism.* Cambridge: Polity.

Davies, W. 2015. *The Limits of Neoliberalism.* London: Sage.

Förster, M., Llena-Nozal, A. and Nafilyan, V. 2014. *Trends in Top Incomes and their Taxation in OECD Countries.* OECD Social, Employment and Migration Working Paper 159.

Frank, R. H. 2011. *The Darwin Economy: Liberty, Competition, and the Common Good.* Princeton NY: Princeton University Press.

Friedman, M. 1962. *Capitalism and Freedom.* Chicago. IL: University of Chicago Press.

Friedman, M. and R. 1980. *Free to Choose. San Diego, CA: Harcourt.*

Harvey, D. 2005. *A Brief History of Neoliberalism.* Oxford: Oxford University Press.

Hayek, F. von 1944. *The Road to Serfdom.* London: Routledge.

Kastner, L. 2017. 'How the finance industry mobilised against the European Financial Transactions Tax', Sheffield Political Economy Research Institute.

Mirowski, P. 2014. *Never Let a Serious Crisis Go to Waste.* London: Verso.

OECD 2015. *In It Together: Why Less Inequality Benefits All.* Paris: OECD.

OECD 2016. *International Regulatory Co-operation.* Paris: OECD.

Ostry, J. D., Loungani, P. and Furceri, D. 2016. 'Neoliberalism Oversold?', *IMF Finance and Development,* June, 38-41.

Piketty, T. 2013. *Capital in the 21st Century.* Cambridge, MA: Belknap Press.

Rand, A. 1964. *The Virtue of Selfishness.* New York: The new American Library.

Slovik, P. 2012. *Systemically Important Banks and Capital*

Regulation Challenges, OECD Economics Department Working Paper 916. Paris: OECD.

Streeck, W. 2014. *Buying Time.* London: Verso.

Streeck, W. 2016. *How Will Capitalism End?* London: Verso.

Social Europe Editon

London, UK

ISBN 978-1-9997151-1-3

Cover design by David McAllister

CPSIA information can be obtained
at www.ICGtesting.com
Printed in the USA
LVOW13s1419111017
552031LV00029B/619/P